# AN OPEN LETTER

# WILLIAM WADE

Published on behalf of SASRA by 10Publishing, a division of
10ofthose.com 9D Centurion Court, Farington, Leyland
PR25 3UQ, England.

Email: info@10ofthose.com Website: www.10ofthose.com

ISBN 978-1-909611-78-8
Designed by Mike Thorpe /www.design-chapel.com

Printed in the UK by CPI

# AN OPEN LETTER

## WILLIAM WADE

Hello there. Thank you for reading my letter, my message in a bottle, which has somehow washed up on your shoreline. However it got to you, I'm glad you've decided to open it. How dull life would be if we never opened shoreline bottles with notes in them or if letters remained closed. So thank you.

I realise I may be taking a risk in suggesting this, but this may very well be unlike any letter you've ever read. At least I hope it is.

All I'd like to do is to share some things with you about that most interesting of topics - life. Life truly is a 'funny old thing', isn't it? I'm sure you've lived long enough to know that already. No doubt you've laughed until you've almost, well, laughed really hard. And I guess you've maybe also cried a bit too, because life is like that - filled with ups and downs, joys and heartaches. I've been there, too.

Let me at least set a little scene for you, to let you know where this letter is being written from. I'm sitting in a holiday home, overlooking a stunning valley of the greenest fir trees, all standing uniformly proud, apart from when they occasionally sway to the rhythm

*As we in a sense journey together, we might learn a little about this strange gift of life as we go.*

of the easy wind. The sky is overcast with threatening greys and silvers, but there's a tiny hint of blue just beyond the furthest trees. I'll not tell you the country, or why I'm here, at least not now. It's just enough for the moment to say I'm happy and I hope that you are in a good place too, both in where you are and in who you are. But I do know that perhaps, as is the nature of life, sometimes we are not. Sometimes happiness eludes us, no matter how much we try, either patiently or ferociously, to catch it. That is why I'm writing this letter, that maybe as you read and as we in a sense journey together, we might learn a little about this strange gift of life as we go.

I must tell you though, this is a letter, and so you might not see titles, headings and the like. Surely we can dispense with the formalities. However best you read – on the train, in front of a roaring familiar fire, in between bringing the kids to and from school, could I suggest you try to find that place where you might be able to relax, contemplate and maybe even find a measure of peace, and let's look at this great, complex and yet simple existence we are involved in - this life we live.

# Here we go...

I don't know about you, but these days, I'm thinking a lot about what I might leave behind when I die. I realise you might well say that that's a very grim place to start a letter, but really, it's not. I don't dwell on death so much as I dwell on what I will leave behind, who I will leave behind, and what impact my life will have had. Of course, there are the usual thoughts of family and close friends who will remember me and the times we've had at various stages of our intertwined lives. But the haunting question, for me at least, is what will I leave the world?

It's a bold question, isn't it? I'm not meaning the whole wide world, of course not. But it might be a good thing to leave a whole bunch of others, apart from my close friends and family a kind of memory, even a legacy, as grand as that sounds. If I could, I would leave something a lot more dramatic than what I am doing right now, which is writing a letter. I would love to be able to leave behind a thriving, well-run, well-kept, well-everything orphanage in one of the poorer

*If I could, I would leave something a lot more dramatic than what I am doing right now.*

countries in the world (or have a 'chain' of them...you know what I mean!). Or I would love to be able to leave behind an iconic speech, caught on camera, like the 'I have a dream' speech, by Martin Luther king Jr., or have been a sporting great, like Rocky Marciano or George Best. But, you see, I'm not really ever going to do that – to leave a legacy like that. I do sponsor two little girls, one in Honduras and the other in Niger, so maybe that's something. It's not an orphanage, but it is something. And I have made many speeches. Even some caught on camera, but I'm not Martin Luther King Jr. And I have done a bit of boxing and a bit of football, but I never found myself in the really 'legendary' bracket! But I did give it a good go.

So, what can I leave the world? Well, as odd as it may sound, I'm leaving the world a letter – this letter, and I'm so glad you're reading it. It's not much, but I guess I'm like a lot of people who do have certain plans, or even dreams, about life. And while I may not have achieved some of the goals I'd hoped I would, maybe as you read this letter, you'll see that sometimes our dreams change as we go along, because we do generally become wiser as we become older, and winning the world heavyweight boxing title could even come second place to seeing your daughter's first nativity play, because life is funny that way.

I didn't really start life with the proverbial silver spoon. Not many do. But like many others, I found a lot of fun in my childhood. As deprived as some might view living on a housing estate with rows of terraced two-up, two downs, there was fun to be had. Just having the freedom as a boy to be running around the jigsaw streets, knowing and being known by everyone, being a part of a real community that looked out for each other was a truly special thing. Front doors were left open in those days, and the 'larger family' feel permeated the estate back then. Of course there were boundaries. We could never stray over to the 'other side', where the children looked just the same as us, but we were told in no uncertain terms that they were very different than us. They were 'dirty' children. Not like us, all clean and Protestant. That's what we were told. And you grow to believe it, because everyone else tells you the same thing. Even the lovely old grannies who were sweetness personified. As a child it becomes your base viewpoint, which touches and taints your framework of thought as a young boy growing up.

I'm the youngest of six, and the only boy. Yes, five older sisters. But can I tell you, it was a wonderful childhood. My five sisters thought I was a gift from God back then, as did my mother and especially my old grandmother, who would have entered me for the 'my grandson is the Messiah' competition, had there been one. My father was proud of me too, I guess. Of course he never said it. Shipyard-working Belfast men never did say things like that back then, but I'm sure he was.

I remember just before we left Sandy Row, where we all bathed in a steel tub in front of the coal fire and had a very scary outside toilet, standing out in the street watching what I thought was another bonfire. I was woken out of my sleep by it, and when I came down to the street, I knew it must have been very late, it was so dark outside, apart from the huge flames. Lots of people around were crying, though, and there was no music. It was one of the houses. Everyone seemed to be blaming the 'drink' and the 'chip pan'. I just knew there were children in that burning house, and everyone stood watching them die, watching the house burn. I was a boy, but even then I knew that there was something not fair about it. Something was wrong. I was angry, but wasn't really sure about what anger was. I would come to know in time. That is my last memory of Sandy Row.

*Something was wrong. I was angry, but wasn't really sure about what anger was.*

We moved out of the city centre to Greenisland. It was another Loyalist housing estate, but the houses were a little more '70s' than '50s'. The incredible attraction of Greenisland was that it actually had a play park, with swings, a great big slide and a 'skateboard' park (which was basically large clumps of concrete placed inside a concrete shell), and it was all very exciting. I'm not sure what you're making of this as you read it, but it was a young boy's dream. It all came to a cataclysmic pinnacle of joy when my grandmother bought me a bike for Christmas, a 'Strika', which was part of the Tomahawk and Grifter range. I was in heaven, riding around that park with my mates, negotiating the 'humps' in the skateboard park on my bike, getting involved in the boxing club, even kissing girls at that tender age. It was all fun. But as I said earlier, life can sometimes be a contradiction, it can be complex. Outside the house, there were adventures and laughter. Inside the house, it wasn't always like that.

As I grew a little older, I soon came to fear weekends at home. My sisters were always fiercely protective of their younger brother, and were never to be underestimated. But honesty demands I tell you that we were all afraid of our father at the weekends. Except for our mother, who was never really afraid of anything. I hope you never had to experience anything like that, but maybe you did. You see, when the weekends came, the drink came too, and when you have a situation where there is a lot of drink, a lot of shattered dreams (which the housing estates back then readily produced) and the typical male propensity for not talking about real issues, then often the dreaded reaction can be expressed through violence. I wish I could tell you that, like the children of Israel in Egypt, that particular curse passed by our door. But it didn't.

*We were all afraid of our father at the weekends.*

My sisters would try to hurry me away from the scene when the rows erupted: this was such a brave and noble thing to do for young girls trying to work out their own understanding of why this was happening in the first place. I wish I'd been shielded from it completely. I wish it had never happened and that we could have been a happy family, with dinners at the table, holidays to the beach and daddy giving us hugs when he came home from work.

My mother bore the brunt of it all. She was a tiny woman, and lived her life for her family, her children. She came from a decent family. Like anyone else she had hopes and dreams of her own, like we all do, don't we? She married my father after six weeks of courting and stayed with him until the day he died. But she paid for her faithfulness. As I said, I wish I'd never seen how my father hurt her, but I did. In all their bravery, my sisters were sometimes just that fraction too late. I hope you've never experienced watching your mother being beaten. As a boy, it did something to me. Apart from instilling an insidious fear of my father in me, it left me with a numbing sense of helplessness, a sense that the bully always wins. That life can often be cruel and there's not a thing you can do about it. Now that is a weighty burden for a child to bear. It forms you, whether you would want it to or not. It infuriates you and weakens you, but it also plants a tiny little seed in you, and that seed is that anger, frustration and weakness can be acceptably expressed through violence. Something I would grow accustomed to not very long after those years.

Perhaps some of what I'm sharing resonates with your own story, your own 'letter'. Maybe you're seeing an image, reliving a memory that you know has shaped you into being the kind of person you are, the character traits that you have, and that you wish you didn't have. The past has a way of leaving its trace with us, even though we fight its very existence, it is still there, still haunting, still flaring up when the pressure is on, still calling and mocking in the darkness of a sleepless night. And sometimes, maybe even most times, we give in, because we grow too tired of fighting. We believe the thought that suggests it's all in the genes and there's nothing we can do about it. It is who we are, might as well face it. A convenient excuse for the demons of our past, and how they still terrorise our present.

*The past has a way of leaving its trace with us, even though we fight its very existence.*

I believed those suggestions as a young boy, because what else was a young boy to do? I couldn't overpower my father, even if I'd had the resolve to do so, which I didn't. I was a child, and he was a man, and not just a man, but my father. I had no brothers, no grandfather. He was the only role model I had, and I revered his hardness, his toughness. I loved how he took on the UDA beating team when they came to break his legs for domestic violence. How he faced them in the back garden and fought with them until he, the bully, was overpowered by other bullies, and that even after the breezeblocks had shattered his knees, he still shouted after them, calling them cowards and that he would see them one by one, once he'd recovered. I loved that about him, I admired it. But like most men, he was a contradiction. That heroism, that solitary bravery was lost on a man who beat his faithful wife, who spent his money on drink and horses, who sold the furniture and went off on 'jaunts' to England, only to return an angry and solemn man a few weeks later. He was both brave and cowardly. The result of his environment, for almost all the men I knew back then walked in the same shoes. But also a result of the little, day-by-day choices he made all on his own. Maybe he also believed that things could never change. Maybe at one time he'd had his own dreams, hopes and plans. And maybe they'd been shattered and he'd settled for the lie, which screamed, 'This is what you are, and this is what you will always be!'

The more I saw, the less innocent I became. The less innocent I became, the more I felt the growing, insidious anger flare and spark inside. The cracks were starting to show. Initially, it came in choosing certain friends over others. I'd always had decent friends as a boy, but now I was seeking out the sons of the other bullies on the estate. They carried a sense of drive, of recklessness that appealed to me. I wanted to be a part of that drive, that pursuit of breaking the boundaries. It was a subconscious moving towards what I felt was not just drive, but pain and anger too. In this, we had a bond. It would never, never be discussed, but we would know it. We admired our fathers, saw them as heroes, but also experienced them as cowards, as monsters even at times. But we honoured them, even though we sometimes loathed them. We wanted to believe in them, but knew that they too were broken. We wanted to be like them, but only the good parts, the heroic parts of them. And we somehow knew that we would eventually emulate them, in all their glory - and yet also in all their brokenness too. It thrilled us and it destroyed us. But we walked the paths they walked. We vowed we would do it better, bigger, stronger. But we knew that fate would have us follow in their shadows. We were their sons. What else could we do?

The same dilemma runs through all of us, doesn't it? The sense that a script, a pre-ordained pathway is destined for us, and no matter how fervently we may try to shake ourselves from it, to stray from those 'ordered steps', we find ourselves continually coming back to that script, that pathway, that feared road that we promised ourselves we would never wander down.

I found myself wandering down the same road my friends were treading on, the same road my father, our fathers, had trod before us. It was a road with painted kerbstones. Red, white and blue. Had I been born in another part of the city, the kerbstones would have been green, white and gold. Had I been born in another part of the world, those kerbstones could have been any colour. The sounds along this road were a mix of chants, marching band tunes, ska, punk and shouts. This road was the familiar, the predictable, the past-becoming-present in a new generation. It was my script, my lot - expected.

By the time I had reached my early teens, the skinhead movement had broken through in Northern Ireland. It had been around for a while in mainland Britain, but now it finally made its way across the water. We all got involved. It was tribal. The culture of the 'pack' permeates our Western mindset, and we eagerly obliged, along with the vices attached. I remember the first night I was offered a bag of glue. Under pressure from older teenagers, and feeling the perceived weakness of refusal, I took it and kept taking it from then on, most weekends.

Glue-sniffing has an underestimated grip on a young life. It seems that in many cities (perhaps due to the fact it is cheaper than alcohol and more potent) these days it is making a comeback. Back then I really enjoyed the high that a bag of glue gave. The taste was somehow appealing, like the disinfectant used on factory floors – clean and pungent. A few breaths of the glue and you would reach a high, a buzz in the brain, a fuzziness of thought. It was enough to stop there, enjoy the buzz and then carry on a few minutes later. But with the glue, another level was possible, the hallucination. If you kept sniffing beyond the buzz, then you would hallucinate. It wasn't like LSD, where your view was psychedelically distorted. You were gone. The hallucinations were mostly disturbing, dark and frightening - almost demonic. But it was the highest level

*Back then I enjoyed the high that a bag of glue gave.*

of high, and why rest at second-best?

As great as we felt the highs were, glue has an ability to sap the life out of you. It causes normalcy to pale into insignificance and so the 'high' is the ultimate in life experience. It won't surprise you to know that my schooling suffered, my desire for everyday life suffered, my worldview, even at that young age, suffered and I became hollow. A teenager who is hollow is both a dangerous and a desperately hopeless person. But what did it matter – we had no other great aspirations in life to cling on to, so if we were to simply live out our days with no real way out of the estate, then why not do it high on glue? That was our mindset, our recklessness, our 'I don't care' attitude. And this attitude began to wind its way through our young lives to the point where it started to become self-destructive.

*Glue has an ability to sap the life out of you... it won't surprise you that my schooling suffered.*

The 'I don't care' attitude is a potentially numbing stance, isn't it? We promise ourselves that 'I don't care' about that relationship, or 'I don't care' about my job, or 'I don't care' about my family, my school, my future, my debts, my addiction, my feelings. But the difficulty with that stance is that really we do care. We do have feelings, and hopes, and a longing for meaningful relationships, and so the 'I don't care' attitude is just a smokescreen, a cover-up, a lie - because we do care. And we do care because we are 'wired' – put together – to care. But life, especially the hurts of life, has a gradual effect on us: the eroding of our emotional attachment to hope: the moving towards the 'I don't care' attitude. For some, it can happen as a crisis moment – the losing of a loved one, being a victim of abuse, the news of terminal illness. For others, perhaps most, it is the culmination of 'little knocks', of the husband who just won't change, the father who is cold and critical, the friend who gradually moves on, the job that destroys aspiration or the world that just seems so uncaring. 'I don't care' is a contradiction. The truth of the matter is, we do care, but we can be forced into a place where we refuse to care, where we allow our consciences to become seared, as if burned by a hot iron, scarred and devoid of feeling. And it's not enough to resign ourselves to the line which says, 'That's life'. For then the creeping, gnawing vines of bitterness, resentment, anger and coldness make their way from our heads to our hearts. And once they wind their way around that, what little hope we may have had of a better life begins to get squeezed from us, like a constricting, suffocating disease, not content until it grips our very souls.

The glue was exciting. I can't tell you it wasn't, for that would be a lie. The highs, as dark as they could be, were also liberating. They were my crushing escape, my moments of hollowing exhilaration. But they came at a cost.

Along with the glue came the drink. It was always going

to come, for it was normality to me. My family culture was steeped in it, the estate was steeped in it, my friends were willing to be steeped in it, and I was only too eager to comply with this familial and peer-driven demand. As physically damaging as it is for a young teenager to be drinking vodka, cider, beer, sherry, and often a mixture of these and others, I always saw the drink as a rite of passage, an acceptable misdemeanour, an applauded sin. You almost heard the subconscious cheer of fathers, of older brothers, of uncles who have taken to the booze at a young age too, lining the road and welcoming you onto the well-trodden path. This was one definite hidden pastime which would not be so seriously looked down on. And the pride of being able to drink a copious amount without passing out added to the bravado. The more you drank, the 'bigger' you were. The more you drank, the 'older' you became. But also, the more you drank, the less you actually fitted into the 'normality' of society, and the more you became a part of a warped cultural trend which limited the true ideals of family values, of genuine friendships, of romantic etiquette, of conflict resolution, of employment expectations, of social interaction and an understanding of acceptable behaviour. Drink takes its toll, although it's not too keen to show its hand in the early stages.

I'm not sure how you view alcohol and its impact on a life. I took part in a university study a few years ago and was faced with the reality that I became what my surroundings dictated I should become. My family drank a certain amount of alcohol, my friends drank a certain amount of alcohol and those in the slightly wider circle of influence drank a certain amount of alcohol, all pointing to a personal viewpoint that alcohol is to be the solace that a person is to turn to in times of happiness, joy, celebration and relaxation, but also in times of pain, hurt, disappointment and brokenness. It is there to enhance the highs in life, and it is there to dull the lows. It is the crutch and the constant friend, the faithful painkiller, but one with a sting in the tail.

I don't want to be judging your life in suggesting how alcohol has damaged my upbringing. I don't know what your relationship is with the booze, but I don't want to make you feel in any way condemned because of how I write about it in my letter. In all I've experienced, I realise that people drink for many reasons, and perhaps in many cases, excusably so. I am not writing from a glasshouse throwing judgemental stones. What I am saying though is that reliance on the drink is ultimately destructive,

*When a person suffers, others suffer too, either directly or indirectly.*

and anything that is ultimately destructive is never only destructive on a personal level. When a person suffers, others suffer too, either directly or indirectly. I don't know how much you might or might not drink. I don't know how reliant or not you might be with the drink. But I do know that very few people view themselves as alcohol-dependant. The drink has an ability to allow the conscience to look at the street drunkard and say 'I'm not that bad'. And when we're not that bad, we don't have a problem. Or so we convince ourselves. My drinking was cultural, shaped and defined by family values, estate values and it was escapist. Was I a young alcoholic? Of course not. But my findings in the university study proved otherwise. Facing truth is not often easy, particularly when it reveals a personal weakness, one which at one point in your life was esteemed as a strength. But it is a worthwhile pursuit – the pursuit of truth.

Mixed with the growing love affair with the drink came a destructively unfortunate alliance with the cultural explosion of the skinhead movement. Already having swept a huge section of mainland Britain's youth, this swathe of anti-authority, coming on the back end of the punk era, reached Northern Ireland in the early 1980s. With the already heaving resentment of the housing estate, the youth of the time were only too happy to embrace a cultural acceptance of anger, violence and rebellion. Being a skinhead was the thing to do.

*Being a skinhead was the thing to do… the youth were happy to embrace violence and rebellion.*

It highlighted a societal boundary that was there to be crossed, the boundary that gave rise to the reactionary, the fractious. Its music and dress gave a permission to clash, to refuse and to be extremely obnoxious in the process.

The insidious part of this journey for me was the underlying ideology attached to the movement. Coming swiftly after the punk expression, which had the symbolism of both badge and patch, the aftermath of the swastika emblem, hailed so prevalently by the Sex Pistols in their imagery, this mixing of what the swastika stood for and the now aggressive movement of skinheads became a potent recipe. It almost normalised Nazi philosophy for a new emerging generation. Of course we didn't know at the time all that the swastika stood for, but we were very happy to daub it on walls, lamp-posts and anywhere else we could use a permanent marker. We were young; we had our right to be heard. But with our youth came a generous amount of naiveté, not that we were aware of it, we felt we knew everything that needed to be known about life, the planet and the universe. But it was slowly getting under my skin.

Isn't it a strange part of life that we can take on ideas and thought systems without actually thinking about them? There is an argument these days that we as a society are blindly following what society dictates. I sometimes wonder if it is not society that is dictating to itself, then reacting to itself by following supposed dictates, but that there may not be a few, perhaps at an educational level, perhaps at a political level (some suggest something even more sinister), who lead these dictates and we, without thinking, follow. That was me as a young man with the Nazi philosophy.

I know this may sound shocking to you. Looking back all these years later, it seems shocking to be sharing it. But there was something, as a young man, angry with life, ready for a thrill, with a little bit of drive (uncontrolled as it was), that led me to hail Adolf Hitler as a hero. Psychologists look at some of the reasons why young men in mid-80's Britain walked the way of the swastika. Apparently a large proportion of it was down to the uniform and regalia. It wasn't with me. There was something sadistically intriguing about the Nazi ideal that struck a chord with me. The strength of leadership, the absolute morality (twisted as it was) upheld by the Nazi party, the mass rallies and stirring speeches, the unswerving commitment to a cause. A cause: that was it! That was the attraction. Looking back on it, I would offer my own psychological spin on it and suggest that young men, particularly in housing estates, need a cause to follow. Now you know as well as I do that that could be a very positive cause or a very negative one. Mine was clearly the latter.

I was learning more about the right-wing cause already in the form of National Front propaganda. I became a member of their cause and received their 'Bulldog' magazine throughout the year. My father was encouraged by the National Front's stance on Loyalist Ulster, but seemed to be unhappy with their racial doctrines. For me, the doctrines all rolled into one. Ulster was British and it should remain so, those who were not British should be forced to leave Britain, IRA members should be executed for either treason or terrorism, Israel should be wiped off the face of the earth. In short, anyone who was not 'WASP' (White, Anglo-Saxon Protestant) should comply with WASP doctrines or be silenced, one way or the other.

This is difficult to share with you. Words on a page can reveal so much, and yet reveal so little. Looking back now, I see a young man needing direction, needing a sense of hope, needing someone to be a father figure who cared, someone who didn't need to see his own father beat his mother at weekends and in the process beat normal social reasoning out of a fractured family. Don't get me wrong, I'm not playing the feel sorry for me card. I chose my thought processes. I guess all I'm asking is that if you ever come across someone like I was back then, perhaps try to see behind what you see. And if you could ever find yourself having the courage to do it (and it's not always recommended), reach out a hand and

*There are people in the world who care... and who don't simply, as a reaction, automatically write someone off.*

see if you might be able to speak a word, show an action that might remind that young man, that young woman, that there are people in the world who care, who do have greater wisdom than they do and who don't simply, as a reaction, automatically write someone off.

The National Front magazine was full of interesting and aggravating stories. It carried reports of black ghettos in Britain, where the whites and the police couldn't go. And if they did, they were beaten, ridiculed and chased. Asian men were forming gangs which picked little white girls off the street and gang raped them. Roman Catholics in Northern Ireland were in league with Jews, trying to undermine the monarchy and reduce the mighty United Kingdom to a joint 'Fenian'/Jewish state. I believed it. I didn't think. I read about Hitler and how as a young man in the First World War he felt hopeless and helpless. His beloved country was

*I read about Hitler and how as a young man in the First World War he felt hopeless and helpless.*

being shamed on the global stage, and he raged against that shame. But he made a decision. He had a dream. He chose to place his anger into a cause. A cause was what he needed, and what he felt the world needed. The emergence of a new kingdom, a new Reich and he would be the Emperor, the Caesar. It was political and social romanticism to a young man who felt shades of Hitler's viewpoints. Ruthless and determined, he would rise and the nation would rise with him. And dissenters? They would face the punishment they deserved – the camps and the gas, the bullet and the experimentation table. I revelled in the stories. I saw myself as the saviour of a blighted Ulster. I felt the call, I had my cause.

It is true that those who advertise during the Super

Bowl each year in the United States realise the power of information to affect actions. I sometimes feel that we as a culture in Britain seem to sit idly by while Jeremy Kyle shapes our understanding of family values, Coronation Street teaches us about relationships, the National Lottery informs us about the value of money and the news programmes instil a morbid sense of fear to undergird it all. It's so easy not to think, isn't it, especially when others seem to be doing it for us?

It was impossible for me to fill my mind with the ideology of Mein Kampf, to devour each issue of the Bulldog magazine, to dream constantly of a revived Loyalist Ulster, to listen to music which encouraged the revolutionary and to be around other young men who were ready to act, without it having an impact on my actions. I should have thought. But instead I dreamed, and that dream was a poisonous one. In those formative years, I found a cause, a dream; a programme of actions which would get me to where I felt was my great calling. Following in the footsteps of Hitler, hearing the whisper of ruthless leadership and destructive progress, having symbol and ideal imprinted on my mind, and by this stage my heart, I found the cause I was looking for – the great dream. I could have called it my mission in life, my destiny. I would become the next John McMichael – Intelligence Officer of the UDA, the Loyalist Ulster Defence Association.

We are often told to be careful what we wish for, aren't

we? I'm not sure of your hopes, wishes and dreams from when you were a bit (or a lot!) younger. Most, if not all of us, hope to be someone, to do something, something great, to be known. At the beginning, the dream is innocent, pure. We want to fly to Mars, to score the winning World Cup goal, to dance the lead in Swan Lake, to be the inspirational leader of a nation. But then comes the reality of life; the hurt, the pain, the facts. And the facts tell us that we will be what we are told we will be. We will not be greater than either our parents or our peers. We fight the facts with the thought that others did it, so can we. But the facts have a grim determination to pester our dreams until we actually become what the facts dictate we become. Maybe that hasn't been your experience, but it became mine. From wanting to be the next Neil Armstrong at age 8 to wanting to be the next Sugar Ray Leonard at age 10, to wanting to be a local celebrity of the violent kind at age 13 to wanting to be the next Adolf Hitler at age 14 to wanting to be the next Intelligence Officer of the UDA at age 16. What happened? The facts won out in the end. And my dream became my drive, my obsession and my path to crossing boundaries. Obsession can do that, can't it? Cause us to do what in normal circumstances we would never dream of doing. But I began to act in a way which became my normality. The 'facts' become truth for us, as twisted as the perceived facts can sometimes be.

My surroundings were shaping my beliefs. And my beliefs

were suggesting some very dark conclusions. I was starting to believe that our Loyalist housing estate was under siege from the Catholics, the Republicans, the scum. They were infiltrating our Protestant context with their Popish ways and thoughts. They were dirty. They were filthy. They were different to us. We were clean, right, upstanding and, what's more, we had God on our side. They had Mary-ology, and the bastardisation of the Holy Bible with their Fenian doctrines. They honoured the Pope as the vicar of Christ, while we, the right ones, exposed him as the anti-Christ. They weren't as intelligent as us and most likely abused their children, just like their paedophile priests were doing. They took the British coin and yet spat their Nationalist venom at the British rule. They bombed our land,

*They were the enemy, but the enemy were on our doorstep. They were ready to fight, and so should I be. So should I be.*

shot our soldiers and raped our women. They were trying to outbreed us and eventually remove the Union Jack from Ulster's shores. They were the enemy, but the enemy were on our doorstep. They were ready to fight, and so should I be. So should I be.

When beliefs get as cloudy as mine were becoming, then with the physical growth of a young man comes a mental growth, the ability to think independently. However, when this ability to think independently is coiled with the weeds of a bigoted mindset, independent thinking is choked by the tribe, by the colours tattooed on the heart, by the thought patterns of family and friends. It becomes you. More than simply an identity, it becomes you. And you, in turn, must act as you believe. Otherwise you are a traitor to your own belief system. You are a turncoat, and worth nothing. So I acted, and acted with the conscience of a Loyalist under siege. What I did was right - but only right in light of a mindset which had been formed by other mindsets of similar persuasion. We were right – that was it – we, the Loyalist people, were right. God was right, and so my actions were justifiable. And so therefore I acted.

At the beginning, like in most new ventures, small steps are necessary to establish further larger steps. I began to take small steps on the road to becoming the pinnacle of what I felt every young man of my sort should be – a freedom fighter for Ulster, and for me, the UDA's leader in 'military' intelligence. The small steps were necessary in confidence-building, in progressing through the ranks, in being somebody. What I am about to share with you I look back on with a sincere depth of remorse. I acted as I felt I should. But now that I am a man, I can say I acted as a prisoner to a tangled dream – a myth. But I acted nonetheless, and here is what I did...

*What I am about to share with you I look back on with a sincere depth of remorse.*

It began with low-level Loyalist territorialism. I have a flair for art. I can draw. I can paint. I have the ability to get the contours, the angles and the shades in proportion. And so I offered my services to the UDA. Local permission was not a necessity. This was not a community project. This was the nailing of the colours to the mast. I equated my murals to the great Martin Luther who ripped into the Holy Roman Church when he nailed his 95 theses to the church door at Wittenberg on the 31st of October 1517. He signalled the death knoll on Catholic doctrine, and I was doing the same on my patch – nailing the red, white and blue around the estate, making the statements and not the suggestions that Ulster (and my housing estate, Greenisland) was marked by the Union Jack, the Red Hand of Ulster and the stamp of a Loyalist God. The simple start was to paint the kerbstones; one kerbstone red, then white, then blue, then red, then on, right until the end of the street. The more Loyalist streets were good starting points. It was easy to garner support from the local residents. They cheered it, it solidified their identity. It helped them in their own way to preach the Loyalist doctrine to themselves every time they looked out into the street – they saw a young man paint their kerbstones with the colours of the Union, and they assented. This was their stand – their fight for Ulster. And I was their active champion – their artist and their voice. I revelled in those beginnings. I was active. Active.

The next step was to take the move towards painting the kerbstones where the sporadic Catholic families were. This was moving into enemy territory, yet territory that I felt needed to be reclaimed by its rightful owners. It came with a touch of nerves, for this signalled the beginnings of drawing the line of 'us' and 'you', of firmly setting the boundaries, of exclusion and inclusion.

Running throughout this early venturing into the 'standing for my cause' journey was an undeniable streak of hypocrisy. As black and white as I liked to believe I was being in this great stand, the truth of the matter was that on our housing estate there were Catholic families whose sons I was friendly with and whose daughters I wanted to be friendly with. In truth, looking back at those families and how they lived on the estate, they must have sat uneasy being surrounded by the Loyalist flags, the yearly bonfires and then the move into being overtly intimidated. The interesting part was that some of those we looked up to in the UDA were neighbours of these families, even friends. My teenage mind couldn't understand it, but then again, I was doing the same. The Catholic friends that I had were real friends, and their families were decent families, and seemingly a lot more tolerant of others' deeply-held beliefs than some of the Loyalist families I knew. I was hypocritical in my approach to the politics of it all. And yet I continued. A lot of it didn't add up, didn't make sense, yet the cause was still driving me forward. And so my conscience was eased

*There were Catholic families whose sons I was friendly with and whose daughters I wanted to be friendly with.*

by beginning to target the marginal Catholic families on the estate, the ones who no-one really got on with, the easy prey. By doing that, I was able to convince myself that I was still doing something for the cause and yet not offending my Catholic friends' families as I was doing it. There's a lot about the Northern Ireland situation that doesn't make sense, but similar mindsets run across the board of society, don't they? The acceptance of the friendly Jamaican family living down the street, having done so for decades, but the rejection of the incoming Romanian family because they're 'not like us'. The acceptance of aborting a child in the womb due to 'circumstances', but the rejection of smoking whilst pregnant. The acceptance of holding the great dream of winning the lottery each week, but the rejection of the capitalist agenda in the City of London. Hypocrisy is easily found, and I was feeding into its demands.

Needless to say, there was an uneasy feeling within the community once the painting really started. The kerbstones began to mark out the impending escalation. In a way I felt like the Fuhrer himself, beginning to increase the boundaries of power, of domination and ultimately of terror. And I enjoyed it.

After the kerbstones, and now that I had got a feel for it, came the murals. As I say, I could paint, and so this would be my next venture. Kerbstones was one thing, a grand statement on a gable wall was another. I was supplied the paint by the organisation and ran a couple of drawings by them. Once the appropriate drawings were selected, I began. The painting was always done at night, but there was always enough lighting around to see what you were doing, to see how the proud masterpiece was coming on.

*This wasn't Michelangelo or Rembrandt. This was the smattering of fears, aggression and pride flung onto a wall.*

I'm not sure if you've ever seen any of the murals painted on walls depicting political stances in Northern Ireland. Some are very amateur, but some are incredibly detailed and I would also say skilled in their appearance. The appearance is one thing, but the intent is another. This wasn't Michelangelo or Rembrandt. This was the smattering of fears, aggression and pride flung onto a wall and it carried with it not only the stance of a political persuasion, but the implicit threat of a forceful affirmation if it would ever be necessary. It was more than a picture on a wall, and I knew it as I painted.

The pictures were variations of the same theme. They often carried the symbolism of Ulster's Loyalist past and present. The Red Hand was often there, although with the emergence of the military exploits of the Ulster Freedom Fighters (as part of the UDA), often the Red Hand was becoming replaced by the more threatening red fist of the UFF. The flags were often present in the murals, the Ulster flag, the Union Jack, the Scottish flag often made an appearance and if the work was more elaborate, the

Welsh and English flags could appear as well, signifying the unbreakable power of the union of the United Kingdom of Great Britain and Northern Ireland. Statements were the real force of these murals. Quis Separabit, No Surrender, For God and Ulster, Remember 1690 and other statements of the same ilk were daubed as the crowning glory declaring why the paintings were there in the first place. Pleas for justice were also made in these murals, such as calling for the reintroduction of internment, or one memorable one which I was particularly proud of at the time, which pictured an IRA terrorist at the end of a hangman's rope, with the words 'Hang IRA Scum' painted underneath. They told a story and fed the thoughts of those who passed by with a persuasion of how they should think, how we should think. How we had better think.

I was a part of the band by this stage, a Loyalist 'Flute Band' as we called them. Again, it wasn't the uniform that swung it for me, it was the ethos, the marching, the taking of ground as the tunes of our fathers were played and we marched in line to the tune, stamping our status with every step, claiming the ground for Loyalism and for King Billy as he defeated the army of Catholic King James II at the battle of the Boyne. We were the Carrick Defenders Flute Band, a respected band within Loyalism and a bunch of men who were tattooed, were funny, seemed to know the ways of the world and were keen to train us youngsters up to follow suit. They played the songs, marched for Ulster, played the field with women and attracted young men like myself to do the same. I played the flute. I learned the tunes. I marched with them and drank with them and started getting tattoos like them. I was becoming them, and enjoying the journey.

The tattoos were another venture into the self-branding that many of us, regardless of where we come from, like to impose on ourselves. It is not necessarily linked to political persuasion or a cause. We want to make a statement, and if we can't do it by natural means, we will brand ourselves to let people know that we stand for something, that we are part of something, or sometimes that we simply exist. It makes people look, take notice.

I have five tattoos; a large colourful dragon, a skull and crossbones with my name underneath, a swift, a bulldog (linked to my National Front allegiance, again with my name underneath – maybe in case I forgot it?) and a Red Hand with the words 'Made in Ulster' around my belly button. I was very proud of my tattoos. I was 'marked' for my destiny. And yet, how I got the money for them shows the continuing hypocrisy of the situation.

Nestled on the edge of a country lane in Greenisland was the Convent. That's right, a Convent – a place where nuns lived. What they all did in there all day and night I had no idea, but I was easily led into imaginations of what they might have got up to. One summer, my friend Jim, another band member, and I knocked at the foreboding door of the Convent and asked if they needed any work done. They said they did and set us to work for the whole summer, clearing pathways of weeds and recovering gravel paths with gravel. They fed us with jam sandwiches and orange juice in the afternoon and paid us £5.00 a week. With that £5.00 a week, I ended up over that summer period getting my Loyalist tattoos. The hypocrisy of it is astounding. Here were a bunch of nuns feeding, watering and paying me and my response is to plaster my body in visual ideologies which refute all that these nuns stood for within the Catholic faith. I hated myself for liking them. But there was little else I could do, for they really were an expression of kindness. It's difficult to argue against that. But my response, as ridiculous as it was, was to think that I had got one up on them, had tricked them into dispensing with 'tattoo money'. It was a great swindle. Or so I thought. I wonder who really got the upper hand.

Another dilemma I was having around this time was the utter genius of an Irish (Catholic) band hailing from Dublin called U2. I was absolutely transfixed with them. Their music was enticing, but alongside that, it wasn't calling for young Catholic men to take up arms against the British Government and people. No, it was actually calling for peace. It did name the event of Bloody Sunday, but the song's closing refrain wasn't to fight

> *I was being directly, through this music, confronted on all that I held as a worldview.*

back, it was simply, 'No more!' The music was appealing, but I was having difficulty. I was being directly, through this music, confronted on all that I held as a worldview. Not only was I being confronted by it, but I was starting to see that it actually made sense – the thought that the violence, the hatred, the bigotry, the ideal, the stance maybe wasn't the greatest path to walk down. And as these thoughts were coming to me and beginning to lodge in my mind, the foundations that had been instilled in me and that I readily embraced were starting to crack, and fracture and splinter. It was as if the dam was feeling the pressure and starting to groan under it. Not just groan, but that traces of water were starting to seep out, ever so slowly. The hypocrisy of despising the Catholic agenda, to the point of increased violence (I had by this time upped my commitment to the 'war' and had gotten to the level of petrol bombing Catholic homes – homes with children in them – which horrifies me as I look back on it now) was shockingly obvious to me. I had Catholic friends, I worked at the Convent for a summer, I fancied Catholic girls. I began to see that I had been programmed by my environment to take on views which were more subjective than objective, more dogmatic than academic. But what could I do? Well, the music was making an argument – be different, break from the crowd, understand that there is a better way. It was challenging and it was charming. And I was beginning to listen.

One of the other serious dilemmas I had to face as an

off-shoot of listening to U2 was in their elevation of Martin Luther King. Their song 'Pride (In the Name of Love)' was exposing a new generation to this eloquent man from the Southern United States. The problem, as I saw it back then, was – he was not white. In fact, worse than that, he was well and truly black. His face seemed generous and his words were like something from another world. He was passionate and intelligent, religious and relevant, strong and compassionate. Looking a little into his life and message as I began to do back then, I found a man who was talking the talk of peace, and not only that, but walking the walk of peace. Beyond his iconic speeches and pleas, there was a man who knew hardship, tyranny, prejudice and hatred. Yet he chose the path of nonviolence and advocated his legion of followers to do the same. He could have gone down in political history as an army General, had he rallied the African-

*Martin Luther King could have gone down in political history as an army General, had he rallied the African-American community to war. But he didn't.*

American community to war. But he didn't. He marched the streets, often amid abuse and attack. He spoke on the love of God for humanity; black and white, rich and poor. He challenged national Government on racial policy, on war theory and on poverty alleviation. He sat with the mothers of lynched sons and called for the response of forgiveness and healing. He made the Bible relevant to everyday life, everyday pain. But I hated blacks. And yet I realised that I didn't know any. In fact the only 'coloured' family I knew on our estate had a couple of daughters that I would easily have liked to have known. And that was tearing me up inside, because once again I saw the hypocrisy, the contradiction, the lie. In fact, I saw the programming. The package of belief was becoming unfurled in listening to this music and discovering this man. It felt as if the foundations were shaking under my young feet.

*It felt as if the foundations were shaking under my young feet.*

Have you ever experienced a foundational fact that you have lived by become, in actual fact, a lie? It can be seen in those families where the adopted child suddenly finds out that she is not 'blood' of the people she has called parents all her life. It can be seen in the disclosure of Government documents which at one time in history may have rationalised a war in which a family member died, believing it was for a 'just' cause. Only to find out that it was anything but. It can be seen in the discovery of a misplaced love, the finding out of an unfaithfulness which can crush the betrayed. We might well all be able to tell our stories of believing one thing when we're young, or immature, or naive, only to wake up to the greater truth when we're older, wiser, or at least a little more world-savvy.

It was around this time that my life really took the turn

which defined the rest of my days, right up to this point. As you read, could I ask you to perhaps put away (if you can) any preconceived ideas about what I will be describing and linking them to your own experiences, if those experiences have been negative. Maybe just open up your mind a little and your heart a lot and come with me as I describe my version of events...

Around this time in my young life, I used to babysit at my sister Carol's house on a Saturday night. I would arrive around 7pm and stay until the kids were put in bed. I never really had to do anything, other than be in the house to make sure the kids were ok. Carol and her partner Davy would then head out to the local 'working man's' club for the night and usually get back in the wee hours of Sunday morning. They would be in jolly mood as they left and would return home, normally with a few friends in tow, in even jollier mood.

The Saturday night routine was usually the same. I would arrive at Carol's on time, stay for around an hour until Carol and Davy left, then the night would really begin. At the end of Carol's street would be about four or five of my pals, with our 'carry-outs'. Around that time I was doing a 10-glass bottle of QC and a few tins of cheap lager. My friends were mostly on the cider, beer and often the most bizarre-sounding Russian-named brand of vodka would make an appearance too. We would have got the carry-out earlier and just waited for the time when Carol and Davy were sufficiently out of sight and for me to signal to the boys that for the remainder of the night, the house was well and truly ours.

The rest of the night normally followed the usual pattern. We would crack open the drink and the craic, as they say, would follow. Banter would be prominent at the beginning. We would wind each other up with the usual derogatory remarks, but never meaning harm at all. We would wonder who might call later (as drunk young souls had a habit of making their way to our welcoming door). We would tease each other about each other's families. They would tell me what they would do with my sisters. I would tell them they would never have a chance. We would discuss the mothers of friends we would fantasise over. We would stay on safe ground with our openness. There was still a guardedness about all we said. It was all kosher according to the rules of the estate. You see I would never reveal my thoughts about the sisters in the token black family on the estate. Nor would I question my Loyalist allegiance and openly wonder if there was an inherent breeding issue at work in all of us. I have no doubt that we all knew these rules, and wondered if we all wrestled with those same questions. Looking back now, I know we did. I know we did.

*There was still a guardedness about all we said... I would never reveal my thoughts about the sisters in the token black family on the estate.*

The music would be on of course. It was usually pretty safe. Ska made an appearance, punk was there too. Simple Minds sometimes made its way on to the little stereo. We were even being exposed to the music of our mate Surgy, who would get us listening to (and lambasting, even though it was catching us) the likes of the B52's, the Cocteau Twins and Sisters of Mercy. But of course we shouted it down. It was all part of the patter. Around 10pm we would order our 'Chinky's', our take-away Chinese meal. It was such a highlight of the night. Chinese food to a drunk young man was just Heavenly back then. It set us up for the night. We would be well-gone by then, and it was like the dividing line between getting drunk and getting completely, as we called it back then, 'blocked'. Pole-axed is probably a better term.

After the Chinky's, we carried on with the drink, the talk, the craic. Sometimes a few other lads from the estate would call and join the banter. We would move on with the drink-talk of girls, of family, of work, of hopes, of plans (always big plans), of fights, of who would beat who, of football, of boxing, of music, of past escapades, of future escapades, of all the usual young man talk; big, bold and brash, filled with confidence and cheers, laced with brokenness, disappointment and fear. It was all there. Yes, it certainly was, as the psychologists and anthropologists say, tribal. And we loved it, for it helped form us. But I wonder in reality if it was just us walking in the footsteps of our fathers before us and of their fathers before them. The scenery changes, the technology changes and the accessibility to opportunity changes. But beneath it all, the tribe is the pull. The belonging is the pull. The drive to be different, yet contradictorily, in the mould of all that is known, is there. As is the aspiration. But so is that communal scream, the fear waiting to be realised. That it will never be different. But as long as we are not different together, we will survive. As raw as it was then, it was there. And we knew it. But it never made the Saturday evening banter. Never.

That was the routine, the Saturday night gathering. It lasted for around a year as far as I can remember. After Carol and Davy returned (we would always hear them coming up the road – noise travels well at night – and the boys would be out the back in a flash), we would leave and head out into the estate, where anything could happen. Meeting a group of drunk girls was always the preferred option. Maybe news of a party would reach our ears. Maybe a scrap might turn out to be the high point of the night/morning. Maybe worse. Anything and everything was up for discussion and experience. We were young after all.

I hope you're getting a picture of how life was around this time. Maybe it is completely alien to you. Maybe you find it hard to picture. Maybe you're understanding every word for it has been your experience to a degree. Or maybe you could have written this story yourself, it's that close to you. But I'm just setting a scene, a life, which ultimately at this point takes a very dramatic turn. A turn which renders me altogether other than what I could have expected or even believed. And it happened right in the middle of one of our little shindigs at my sister's place on a Saturday night, drunk and revelling with my mates.

Ok, here goes. As I said earlier, open your mind a little and your heart a lot, for this is a story which is not only precious to me, but may even have an impact on you too. I truly hope it does...

The date was April 4th, 1987. It was Saturday night again, and it was around 9 or 10pm. The drink, the craic, the banter and the music were all in full swing. It was going to be another drunken evening, another gathering of ourselves together to cajole, to defame, to laugh, to hope and to pass from young men enduring the passage rites of the estate into older men dictating those passage rites to those who would follow.

*Then came the knock at the door. That in itself was not a surprise, that little house had many knocks on the door on a Saturday night.*

Then came the knock at the door. That in itself was not a surprise, that little house had many knocks on the door on a Saturday night in those days. Nor was it a surprise to see two girls there asking to come in. They wouldn't have been the first to come in on a Saturday night and we would have hoped they wouldn't have been the last. They had what would now be classed as typically estate names; Sandra and Tracy. They were just 15 years old at the time. We were aged between 16 and 18. So they were cordially invited in.

I'm not exactly sure what any of us were expecting from these two girls. They were certainly young and pretty and in our age range, but it became suddenly apparent that they were not there to be won over by any Romeos in the room. They had a story to tell.

As the music was blaring out of the corner, and as we as young men spoke a lot louder, like strutting peacocks in order to be heard and to impress, one of these girls walked over to that little stereo and turned the music off. Now that was quite a brave move to make. They could easily have found themselves out on the street after a move like that. But they clearly wanted to catch our attention. As if simply being there wasn't enough to do that.

What they then began to tell us took us completely by surprise. Well it certainly took me by surprise. These two 15-year-old girls stood as bold as brass in the centre of that living room, aware of who they were speaking to, and began to tell us their story. Now, outside of all that they began to tell us, we knew their families. We knew their brothers. Their brothers were years ahead of us on our journey into estate manhood, and we wanted to get there as fast as we could. These girls came from families like ours, with all of the same hopes and heartbreaks, all of the same joys and fears. And here they were, saying something to us from what seemed to be a different planet. But they were saying it anyway, and how they said it.

They began to talk to us of being 'saved' and 'born-again', of giving their hearts to Jesus and of being forgiven, of being 'assured of an eternity in Heaven' and of 'escaping an eternity in Hell', of having joy and peace and of knowing God as their father and their friend. They waxed eloquent for what seemed like an era and left us stunned as to what exactly was going on. Of course we were aware that this was April Fools' Day. Was this some kind of a joke? Was there a secret camera somewhere? Were these girls going to crack and laugh and say that they were only kidding and could we share our vodka with them? But they didn't crack and they didn't laugh. They were as serious as they were energetic.

*They began to talk to us of being 'saved' and 'born-again', of giving their hearts to Jesus and of being forgiven.*

The next thing was almost absurd. They performed a drama right there in the middle of the room for us. A drama! It was of a boy and a girl and they seemed very much in love, but the boy ends up breaking the girl's heart. She then gives her heart to Jesus and he makes it all brand new again. And they did this to us. They performed this to tell us something.

They of course went on to direct all of this towards us and our lives. They challenged us to get saved too, to give our hearts to Jesus so that he could make our hearts brand new again. They told us that God loved us, I mean that he really loved us. And not only that, but that he loved us so much that he sent his son to die for us on a cross to take the punishment of our 'sins', which we should each be punished for. But Jesus took it. Because he loved us. Because God loved us. Us.

*They challenged us to get saved too, to give our hearts to Jesus so that he could make our hearts brand new again.*

They left the house shortly after their evangelistic foray into our darkness. But they left with a direct challenge; that we should go to church with them the following evening. That we should go to their 'Gospel Service'. Feeling a little perplexed and not a little uncomfortable, we all cried that surely we would go, and ushered the girls out into the dark night again. In the hope that they would never return. We gathered ourselves with a few derogatory quips and resumed our original intention for the evening; to get as drunk as we possibly could and to take ourselves out into the estate once my sister came home again. And that we did.

The next day was an ordinary Sunday. I woke without a hangover as I did in those days and we gathered together on the estate to talk over the previous night's events. Sundays on the estate were calm and slow. It felt as if the estate was like a resting giant on a Sunday, and we didn't want to wake it. So we talked and walked and stood and sat around the estate on a Sunday. This Sunday had another little surprise in store for us though. Around 6pm, while we were standing at the corner of Gortlane Drive, who should appear but our very own estate angels, Sandra and Tracy. They saw us and made a bee-line straight for our little group of around seven. They proceeded to tell us of our promise to turn up at their Gospel Service and we proceeded to tell them why that was not going to happen. The ensuing problem was two-fold; firstly, they would simply not quit on getting us to their meeting and secondly, one of our own number came up with the questionably bright idea that as we were not doing anything else, it might be a bit of a laugh if we go and at least we could disrupt their tiny Christian gathering. It would be a bit of fun to liven up the early evening. So that kind of settled it. We went. We all marched down to that little church like a Corps of the Salvation Army on a mission. Only our mission wasn't so noble.

Around 6.30pm, we walked into the little Jubilee Hall on Greenisland estate. The hall was a Nissan Hut, reminiscent of old Second World War movies. It was old and tired, even then. The main room had wooden floors and electric heaters on the side walls. The chairs which were wood and metal were laid out in rows, and there were chairs enough for around thirty people. That night, there were approximately twelve there, old and young. At the front was Stephen, nicknamed Ben, who was playing guitar and who had a colourful past himself. The women all seemed to be wearing French beret-style hats. Not all did, but the berets were definitely out in force.

Of course we all sat at the back, filling their back row and almost doubling their attendance. I sensed that our arrival caused a little stir and you could almost taste the expectancy of 'fresh meat' for the evangelical kill. We would soon reassure them otherwise. The songs were lively and well-sung. They were an enthusiastic bunch, even though they were small in number. They clapped their hands. So the only thing to do was for us to give the obligatory nods and for us to join in and to clap our hands too. It was a bit of a laugh, after all. During the 'in-between-bits' and the prayers, we nudged and whispered, making various sounds and pointing. We kicked chairs and sniggered, all the while wondering what kind of a bizarre little world we had just walked into. The rising sense of the little flock's discomfort at us being there began to be felt. We were no longer fresh meat, but a veritable pain in their religious necks. The difference was, they cared about their little meeting. And we didn't. But as the great quote from earlier had stated, we weren't doing anything else, so why not? What harm could it do to us?

In a strange twist of events, I expected the greatest heckling to take place as soon as the preacher stood up to preach. That was the defining moment of this little gathering, and if there was ever a moment to disrupt a meeting, it was then. We could verbally destroy this man in the suit at the front. Easily. But the most unusual thing happened. He stood up to speak, and for a start, I was expecting a posh, educated, professional minister with talk and an accent that would fly over our young estate ears. His opening line, looking directly at us was, "You're all sinners!" What a great start to the night. We could have fun with this boy. But then he went on to say, in a disarming accent as broad Belfast as you could get, "But I want you to know that God loves you."

Words are sometimes so incredibly limiting. I would hope to convey to you what kind of a deep-rooted impact that phrase had on me as soon as those words flew from that man's mouth. But I simply can't. I am neither Wordsworth nor Shakespeare. But I even wonder if either of those two could describe the earth-shattering lightning bolt to my soul those words produced. Here was a man, a man I discovered later to be a former East Belfast bar manager, who had friends in all the wrong places, who had mixed with men I esteemed as Loyalist heroes, who could 'handle himself', as the saying goes, who was not afraid of us, who seemed as genuine as he was passionate and who was not trying to pull the wool over our estate-tinted eyes. Here was a man who was saying something different, something extraordinary, something

*Here was a man who was saying something different, something extraordinary.*

powerful and something directly to us – to me.

I guess one of the reasons that the idea that God loved me was so shocking was simply because of me. Because of what I had become and where I was heading. You see, I don't know about you, but I kind of had the thought that if there ever really was a God, then he would never be interested in the likes of me. He would be interested in good people, in honest and upright people. I had the notion that Christians were, and I'm aware that this might sound a little odd, people who were from the right side of the tracks. People who had jobs. People who had houses and gardens too. People who had fences around those gardens and who did well in school. People who went on holiday every year and who wore smart clothes. People who looked down on people like me. People who had a car and who stuck at things. People who went to church and baked cakes for jumble sales. People who were different to me.

*One of the reasons that the idea that God loved me was so shocking was simply because of me... of what I had become and where I was heading.*

But here was this man, who sounded even rougher than me and could have been on an accentual par with the roughest on the estate, telling me of a God who isn't interested in what kind of house you own, or whether you even have a job or not, whether you did well in school or were an academic failure, whether you had smart clothes or not, whether you had been brought up in church or not.

This man was saying that God is interested in the heart, in giving over everything to him, the weaknesses, the fears, the failures, the anxieties, the sins, the anger, the resentment, the bitterness, the prejudice, the sectarianism, the violence, everything. And what's more, God will not only take that from us, if we 'repent', but he will give us, give me, a completely new heart, a new start, a new beginning, a new life.

He went on to tell of this great historical event of the cross, and of Jesus, and of the 'shed blood' of the son of God in order to pay the penalty of our sins, every one. Every one. And even though it seemed to be a completely new language, a new vocabulary, I knew what he was saying. I understood completely. I got it. The best way to describe what was racing through my mind was that there was another voice behind this man's voice, instantaneously explaining everything I was hearing. It was a revelation, a discovery. It was as if God was actually communicating something of his own story to me. To the one who just wanted to destroy, to break down, to maintain the divide. This young man who was caught up in a lifestyle that was heading towards self-destruction, either by political involvement in my surroundings or by self-loathing due to the hypocrisy of everything I was experiencing around that time.

God loves me. I was finding it difficult to get beyond that phrase alone. But wave after wave of new information was coming hard and fast at me. The death of God's son on my behalf, the promise of a new life, the offer of forgiveness, the exclusive demand of being a disciple, the expectation of repentance, which would entail a turning away of my self-destructive lifestyle. It was as if Heaven itself was opening up before me as I sat on that hard chair, offering, beckoning me to come in and to be a child, a friend of God, of the creator of the universe, of the only true being in existence, of the one who died to 'set me free' as I was being told.

At last the evangelistic whirlwind was over. A song was sung to finish and we all shuffled our way outside, back out into the cold reality of the estate, our stomping ground and our identity. As expected, we laughed about all that took place. We joked about the silly hats, about the crazy songs, about the preacher who should be in the next Blues Brothers movie. It all became banter. We moved on. But I couldn't. The truth was, I was gripped by a nagging realisation. Something actually happened in that little room. On the outside, it was just a quaint, almost other-worldly Christian meeting that I had just experienced. But underneath that surface experience was something a lot deeper, something which touched the core of my being. The sharp, direct words of that preacher were sticking to me like biblical glue, like a holy awareness of God, and not only that, but of a God who it seemed loved me. And loved me like no other. Loved me enough to pay the price of my horrific lifestyle choices, loved me enough to offer me forgiveness for all of that junk I was involved in. Loved me enough to plead with me to be rescued from the direction I was heading in. As the preacher said, loved me enough to forgive my sins and to save me. I was laughing with the others, but inside I was shaking with a conviction that I needed to get right with God. That I needed to join this merry band of believers. That I needed to be saved.

For the next two weeks, the greatest inner turmoil I had ever experienced took place. I wrestled with so many relevant thoughts. I wondered about all I had heard. I heard it all again the following Sunday, for even though we all carried on as usual on the following Saturday night, the next evening, we decided to return to the quaint little church, 'just for another laugh'. It was the same again. Saturday night, drunk and big talk. Sunday night, some banter and joking in the meeting (although a little more reserved) and pin-drop silence while the preacher, Tommy,

*It was the same again. Saturday night, drunk and big talk. Sunday night, some banter and joking in the meeting and pin-drop silence while the preacher, Tommy, let loose on us young tearaways.*

let loose on us young tearaways. He repeated his message. Of course, the references, the stories, the applications and the points were different, but it all came down to that shocking statement; God loves you. Yes, there was still the talk of repentance, of turning away from our lifestyles, of giving up 'the world and its ways'. But all of that made perfect sense, because if Jesus really did do this great act for us, for me, then wasn't giving him my life (whatever that was worth) the least I could do in return? And anyway, the things I was being challenged to give up were actually the things that were ultimately damaging in the long run. It actually made sense.

But of course there was a problem. And the problem again was me and everything associated with me. For a start, I didn't believe I could just shout 'Hallelujah' and easily walk away from everything I had known up until that point. What would happen if I decided to become a Christian on the Sunday night and the following Saturday couldn't resist the urge to go partying again, to get my carry-out and to chase the girls? What about the court case I was involved in and ongoing for assault and criminal damage? People would just think I was looking for a get-off ticket. What about my feelings of political idealism and my great dream of becoming the next John McMichael? What about my friends, would I have to give them up as well as everything that was deemed to be bad in my life? Could I be weaned off the drink or would it be a 'Eureka moment' that would rid me of it? What would

*But of course there was a problem... I didn't believe I could just shout 'Hallelujah' and easily walk away from everything I had known up until that point.*

my father think of all this, my mother, my sisters? The sense of God calling to me was so very real. But so were the doubts, the questions, the wrestling.

We had gone to two Sunday night services at this little church and it felt as if my world was going through the washing machine. Everything was swirling everywhere all at once. There were genuine thoughts of God, then genuine thoughts of "Wise up, William!" It was all so very intense, so very real and exciting, yet troubling and scary.

After that second Sunday evening meeting, a few of us met with Sandra and Tracy in Tracy's family house. It was an estate house, just like ours and it was a Thursday. We were in the living room and it was all very serious. It had to be. Big decisions lay in the balance. We began to bombard the two girls with question after question. We asked about what we needed to give up (always a searching and poignant question for a young man to ask), why Christians dressed the way they did, why was everyone at the church so happy, what was Tommy and his wife Margaret's story, could God really make young men like us Christians, would we have to give up football, was there football in Heaven, what was Heaven like, does everyone go to Heaven when they die, does the church just want our money (not that we had any!), and so the questions went on.

The majority of our interrogation ended up being around the subject of eternity, of Heaven and Hell. These two girls clarified in no uncertain terms exactly what Tommy had been banging on about in those meetings, that there was a 'Heaven to gain and a Hell to shun'. It seemed that anyone who did not commit their lives to Jesus Christ and become born-again would eventually spend eternity in Hell. Those who committed their lives to Jesus Christ and became born-again would eventually spend eternity in Heaven. This made logical sense to my young mind, as a decent judgement on humanity would seem to be that if anyone does not want to spend their life with God in their lifetime, then why would they want and expect to spend eternity with him in the life to come. Likewise, if a person committed their life to following God while they lived, then wouldn't God welcome that person into Heaven when they died? Theologically of course it was more than this simple logical equation, but it seemed to make sense.

Beyond the logic though, there was something else. Logical reasoning is great, but it can only reach a certain point. I believe it takes something more to win the heart, especially when it comes to religious matters. The real issue for me was this; as those two girls spoke about Heaven, they did so with such a certainty that astounded me. Now of course anyone can be passionate about their beliefs, but my experience was such that it was as if they, just like Tommy, in those moments when they spoke of Heaven, of no more sorrow, no more pain, of joy and peace, forever and ever, never stopping, ever, that I once again sensed a voice beyond their voice. It was as though Heaven almost came and touched us in that little housing estate living room. No, there were no choirs of angels, no violins in the background. There was something even greater. There was a tangible presence of peace. I mean tangible, not just the absence of fear of anxiety, but a real, almost what I would have imagined holy to have felt like, presence. And it was phenomenal. It was real.

What that living room interrogation did for me that Thursday afternoon was to cement the argument for me. When I left that house, the wrestling stopped. The inner turmoil was over. I decided that day that I was going to the meeting on Sunday night and come what may, I would take the almost unbelievable stand of becoming a Christian.

Saturday night came and went as usual. This would probably be my last drinking session with my mates. I might never have the same relationship with them ever again. I might lose them. But I was actually ready for that choice, ready to make a stand for Jesus, in light of all that I had heard about how he had made the ultimate stand for me.

*I might never have the same relationship with my friends ever again. I might lose them. But I was ready for that, ready to make a stand for Jesus.*

Sunday night came. I began to get nervous. That peace and inner rest I had experienced since Thursday started to shake a little, and by the time the meeting came around, I was wrestling, and wrestling hard once more. We all went, the seven of us. We joined in the choruses. We laughed a little, but my response was more half-laugh, half-serious. Kind of like that face you pull when you hear a bad joke. Tommy stood up to preach. It was Easter Sunday, 1987. Tommy preached his heart out on the cross and the resurrection. Once again, he laid it on thick to us boys and challenged us to respond, to get right with God, to be saved.

It seemed that he had no longer started than he had finished. This was it. Crunch time. The way this little church ended its sermons was to get everyone to close their eyes and bow their heads, and for Tommy to ask, while everyone is head-bowed, with eyes closed, if there might be someone, anyone, who would like to commit their lives to Jesus. If there was, then that person was to signify that decision by raising their hand so that Tommy could see it. It was laced with the reality that this raising of the hand didn't save anyone, it just indicated that after the service, Tommy would lead that person in a 'prayer of repentance' and that would be the moment of salvation.

And then he stopped. And waited. It felt like my heart was going to burst out of my chest. You see, I hadn't shared my thoughts with my friends. They didn't know. All though the service and certainly at that moment of decision, everything went through my mind once more. What would my friends really think, my father,

*And then he stopped. And waited. It felt like my heart was going to burst out of my chest.*

60

my family, would they disown me, what about my future, where did it lie? As I struggled over all of these thoughts it was as if I had a glimpse of what life would be like if I lost this moment, if I let it slip by without responding. I tried to picture my life 5 or 10 years down the line, into my early and late twenties. What would it be like. And the truth of the matter was that I didn't need much imagination to come to a prophetic conclusion on it. My life would be exactly what all the other twenty-somethings on the estate were like. I would be another version of my father. I would be a carbon copy of my friends. I would become what the estate and my upbringing were dictating I would become. I had proven that already. Time would simply confirm the trajectory of my life. Because I was truly powerless to do anything else. Of course I could try, but I'd tried before. It was as if my life followed the pattern of being confined to the shadows of my father's ideals and beliefs. Whether I liked it or not, that was where I was heading. The cast was set. And I didn't like it. I wanted out. I wanted something different for my life. And I finally came to the point where I realised that what I wanted more than anything in that moment was for God to came and make me his son, his disciple and his friend. Not caring what my friends would think, what anyone would think, I started to lift up my hand. Then the strangest thing happened. I saw out of the corner of my eye (I was looking at the ground while all of these thoughts were bombarding my brain) and my friend

Ian raised his hand. I couldn't believe it. He never told me he was going to do that! About three seconds after Ian raised his hand, I also raised my hand. Then another friend raised his, and right at the end, another friend indicated that he wanted to become a Christian too. I did it! I made the giant leap, and I can only say that I was filled with the greatest excitement I believe I had ever had in my life.

There were hushed sounds of "Amen" and "Hallelujah" around that little hall that night as we responded to the call of salvation. We were later to find out that three of those older ladies with the berets decided to pray on a daily basis from that first night we arrived into that hall until the time when we might one day get right with God. They warred for our souls. We never knew them at that point, but we later found out that they were mighty prayers. It was almost as if we never stood a chance! It seems that God takes very seriously the prayers of his saints. Particularly older ladies with berets!

*There were hushed sounds of "Amen" and "Hallelujah" around that little hall that night as we responded to the call of salvation.*

As soon as the meeting was officially over, the four of us were brought in one by one into a tiny side room, no bigger than a broom cupboard really. Tommy explained very carefully to us that we needed to change if we were going to make this decision. But he also told us that once we gave our lives over to Jesus Christ that the Holy Spirit would be our helper, our 'Comforter' as Tommy referred to God's Spirit, and that he would guide us, strengthen us and be our indwelling power. This was a genuine comfort to me, for I wondered whether I could make it as a Christian. This promise made a world of difference to my young mind. Once Tommy was assured that I was serious and not playing around with this decision, he led me in that prayer of repentance. I never knew how to pray, so Tommy would pray a line and I would repeat it, but only if I was in agreement with what was being prayed. I was. It went something like this...

"Heavenly Father, thank you for sending your son Jesus to die on the cross for me. I believe that he died and rose again and that his blood can wash away all my sins. I ask you now to forgive me of all the wrongs that I have ever done. Would you come in and save me? Would you make me born-again? Would you fill me with your Spirit and give me the strength to live as a Christian? I trust you now and confess that Jesus Christ is Lord of my life. I believe that I am saved and that you will be with me all the days of my life. I turn away from my old life of sin and turn to follow you. Give me the strength to be a witness for you and to tell others of what you have done for me. In Jesus' name. Amen."

It was simple, but it was honest. It was short but it was enough. It was direct but it was profound. I had given my heart, my life to Jesus Christ. As much as I have tried to articulate it in a far greater way, the only real way I can describe how I felt after I prayed that prayer, as honestly as I could, was that I felt clean inside. For the first time in my life I felt clean inside. And I knew the difference between clean and dirty. So many times up to that point I had felt dirty, unclean, sometimes just downright filthy inside. But now, after giving over my life to Jesus Christ I felt clean. Truly clean.

I walked out of that hall that evening a different young man. I felt that the hatred had gone. The drive for self-destruction had gone. The anxiety of the upcoming court case disappeared. The need to prove myself vanished. I was a Christian, a believer, a disciple. I was a child of God. And even though I wasn't exactly sure how, I just knew that everything was going to be ok. Yes, everything would work out ok. Because God was with me, and I was unashamed to say that I was with God.

Well, that's my story. My letter. My legacy to the world. To you. Maybe you saw it coming. Or maybe it took you a little by surprise. It certainly took me by surprise!

It might be a little too intriguing to leave my story just there. As if I simply wandered off into the sunset and all was well. That might leave too many unanswered questions. For instance, what happened directly after my sudden conversion? How did my life pan out? Did I keep the faith? How did my father react? Did my friends make it? What am I doing now, over 25 years later, has it really worked out ok?

Well, maybe just to finish this letter off, I'll try to answer some of those questions for you. It won't take long, and it might be in some way inspirational. I hope so.

As you can probably imagine, I didn't ride into an eternal sunset and experience joy and peace for the remainder of my days. What I did have was an assurance that God was real and that he would help me from there on in. The rest I left into his hands. There was, of course, some joking from friends, but actually nothing so serious as to cause me to waver. I wonder if, deep down inside, those friends who were giving me a bit of friendly grief may have genuinely wanted me and my newly-converted friends to stick at it, so that it might give them a measure of hope for their own future. Kind of like using us as religious guinea pigs to see if this Christian thing worked. So there was a bit of jibing. But only a bit.

*As you can probably imagine, I didn't ride into an eternal sunset and experience joy and peace for the remainder of my days.*

Tommy was very astute in that this little church used to do a Tuesday night 'open air service' around the estate. And one of the first things he did was to get each of us to give our 'testimony' at this open air service. We were to tell our story, in front of all of our friends who used to casually come within earshot, about how Jesus had saved us and set us free. It was a nerve-wracking step to take, but I now see Tommy's wisdom in it. He was getting us to nail our fledgling Christian colours to the mast at the very start, and it was such a helpful initiation into being an 'open' Christian, rather than a closet one.

My family's reaction was an interesting one. I deliberately chose not to tell my family straight away, I felt that if I really had changed, then they would see it and that would confirm any decision they might hear about on the estate grapevine. But I didn't have to wait to prove my revolutionary lifestyle to them. It seemed that almost immediately my family heard of my conversion. My mother was elated. I guess she saw her son begin to walk a very familiar journey, a journey that she would have given all she had to protect me from. So when she heard I had become, as the phrase sometimes went back then, 'good living', she was overjoyed.

My father was less enthusiastic about my great decision. In fact he didn't like it at all. He argued that we had a religion anyway, the Protestant religion and that I didn't need to become 'soft'. I later found out that my father's displeasure was more to do with fear than with religious grievance. He was afraid that because news had gotten around the estate that I had become a Christian, that the estate would be a very unforgiving place for me and that I would be harassed, picked on, maybe even bullied. And he was afraid for that. But of course he could never say that to me. He could never be afraid. It wasn't the thing to be. Maybe he just felt that his dreams of me being somebody in the Loyalist ranks, or of me being something to be overtly proud of slipped away when he heard I had become a Christian. However it translated into the mind of this hardened man, he was not happy. And he let me know that.

My sisters took my mother's stance on it, and I suppose hoped that I would definitely not become an 'estate man'. They had seen their fair share of how estate men could be and the thought that their only brother would become one placed a certain amount of fear into their own hearts for the future of their youngest sibling. They were happy for me, and I knew it.

The next few years proved to be trying ones. Initially I grew into my Christian faith rapidly, reading the Bible, discovering incredible things in there, going to all the Christian meetings I could, trusting God for my present and of course my future. It was all new, fresh and exciting. It was a completely new life. I was telling my story and enjoying doing that. Maybe God could help me to see others make this great decision that I had made. Wouldn't that be incredible?

*I had left school with nothing. And had broken my mother's heart in doing so.*

Unfortunately, those early days also saw me make what I felt was a gross slip-up, and once which I almost never recovered from. I had left school with nothing. And had broken my mother's heart in doing so. I threw everything the educational system offered me back into their snobby faces. That was how I saw it back then. So by the time I became a Christian, I was working on one of the popular government training schemes, earning £25.00 per week. There was a young man there working alongside me called Mark who I had crossed swords with in the past and he had come off worse in that encounter. Now that I was a Christian, he decided to push the boat a little, to see if I would really turn the other cheek. So he started. First, it was just jibes, name-calling and mockery. It persisted, but I held firm. Then he upped the ante and started to push a little bit. Just a little, but I remained calm, trying as hard as I could to indeed, turn the other cheek. But then one day he must have felt incredibly brave and he decided to have a go. He had been on at me all lunch time and I was tired of it. He pushed me, and I was embarrassed. So I pushed him back. As I pushed him, his face changed, and you know when someone is going to swing for you. After being forced to take those few steps back, he quickly rushed at me. His body language, his face, told me that he was going to have a crack at revenge. I had to make a snap decision. I was a Christian. What should I do? I decided that to hit him in the face was a terribly un-Christian thing to do, so I hit him a body shot, a right hook just under the heart, and down he went. And out I walked. I walked out of that government training scheme right there and then and thought that God hated me. That I could never really become a Christian and that I had let God, my family and the church down. That I really was destined to become my father's son after all. I went straight out and got some magic mushrooms to take away the pain of failure.

Looking back on it now, I realise how foolish I was. I was so harsh on myself. God didn't hate me. He was there to forgive me. So, I'd slipped up, but I was just coming out of a troubled background, one in which I would have not only cracked this other young boy, but done some damage while he was on the ground. So I had at least progressed from that. But all I saw was failure. How could I be a Christian and have hit someone? Had I really changed at all? The truth was I had, but my own misperception

> *Looking back on it now, I realise how foolish I was. I was so harsh on myself. God didn't hate me. He was there to forgive me.*

was that I thought I had to be perfect. Of course no-one is perfect, but that was my expectation. A false expectation. So I went back to my old life for a while. And couldn't stand it. I really was like the Prodigal Son, wanting to go back to my father, but thinking I couldn't. Thankfully I eventually came to my senses and at the age of 19 recommitted my life to Jesus Christ, realising that I was truly forgiven for not only that slip-up with Mark, but also on turning my back on God. How forgiving is the love of God! And I have been walking with God ever since.

I eventually ended up serving seven years with the Royal Irish Rangers/ Regiment in Germany, England, Saudi Arabia, Kuwait, Bahrain and Northern Ireland. I was the

Regimental Welterweight Boxing Champion and became known as the 'Punching Preacher'. It was while in the army that I preached my first sermon, in Saudi Arabia, on the subject of 'You Must Be Born Again', from John's Gospel, to around 100 soldiers. I also went on to complete a 2-year residential mission training school in Northern Ireland, which is where I met Tulsi, who would later become my wife. Still later, I felt 'called' into the work of SASRA (the Soldiers' and Airmen's Scripture Readers Association) and my wife and I ended up being missionaries with this organisation which is the sharing of the Christian message to British Forces. For us, we were sent out to Germany, and after 12 years, we are still out here serving with SASRA.

So God has been as faithful as that preacher Tommy said he would be. From someone who was self-destructive and bitter, I have now become a messenger of the forgiveness and peace of God through Jesus Christ. From someone who was a hopeless case, someone who was told by a policeman one night in a police cautioning room that I would be 'a waster for the rest of my life', I have become a missionary for the greatest news of the greatest person ever told. From someone who left school with nothing, I have since gone on to gain a Diploma in Biblical Studies, a Degree in Theology, a Master's Degree in Theology and am currently completing a PhD in Theology. From someone who found it difficult to hold down a job and a relationship, I have now been in full-time Christian service for 12 years and have been married for 16, and blessed with two absolutely adorable girls, Micah (8) and Esme (5). From someone who had an almost phobic fear of public speaking, I have been given a strength and an ability beyond myself to have spoken of my faith to tens of thousands. From someone who feared the future, I now look forward to all that God has in store. Am I perfect yet? Far from it! But the

*The great news is that God has promised to keep working on those who commit to him.*

great news is that God has promised to keep working on those who commit to him, those who are serious about being his disciples. It is not easy, but it is worth it.

Of my friends who made their commitment to follow Jesus Christ the same night I did, two are still going on with God and one is not. The one who is not went fairly quickly back into his old ways and continued to walk the path that so many others from the estate walked. The interesting thing is, knowing him and having spoken with him over the years, I know that he would love to 'come back to the fold' so to speak, but feels it is just out of reach. Probably like I felt when I walked away from Christianity, like a let-down to God. But I know that he knows that God is only a prayer away. So I have hope for him.

Alan went on to keep walking with God. Also from an estate house, he ended up becoming a tradesman, marrying Janet, also a committed Christian, and they live with their three children not far from the estate. They still worship at a church on the estate and their heart is to reach those who were just like us. Without God and without hope. God has blessed them and kept them and infused them with that same missionary heart from the early days of our walk with God.

Ian went on to marry Tracy, one of the two doorstep evangelists who knocked on our door that fateful Saturday night. Ian also went on to become a tradesman and they live on the estate with their three children. They are still walking with God and a vital part of the local church and are a witness to the saving power of Jesus Christ.

*It is just not easy to walk with God in this world. It is much easier to follow the crowd than to follow the Bible.*

Sandra kept the faith for a while, but eventually went back to her old ways also. We still keep in contact and she would desperately love to be as she was back in those days of being a young missionary for God. But again, feels that she has let God down and perhaps that God is angry with her. Of course she knows that God would love nothing more than to have Sandra back following him. But as I said earlier, it is just not easy to walk with God in this world. It is much easier to follow the crowd than to follow the Bible. Easier to go along with everyone else than to stand up for Jesus Christ.

Of my friends who didn't decide to follow Jesus and be saved, all went according to the rules of the estate. I'm sorry to say that some ended up in Jail for manslaughter, some ended up being heavily involved on a leadership level within Loyalist Paramilitary life and others just went on to have a fairly normal, everyday existence on the estate, and seem happy to have done so.

My father and mother are both gone now. My father never really came to terms with my decision to become a Christian. There was a turnaround though. As 'soft' as he felt I had become, something happened which changed his mind on that perception. I was involved in a mission, a one-week series of evangelistic meeting in the Greenisland Community Centre. The mission had been well-publicised. The subjects of each talk were headlined on the invitations. They asked questions and sought to provide answers. One of those talks was on the subject of, 'Protestantism, Catholicism and the Emptiness of a Dead Religion.' More than the other talks, this one set some tongues wagging, and caught the interest of the local Loyalist working man's club, who promised to send some 'boys' up to hear what was going to be said. I got the clear impression that if I was going to knock the Protestant faith then I was going to be knocked a little myself. The drama of it all spread around the estate. On the night, there were a few extra 'boys' there who were very intent on what they were hearing. I preached about the fact that in Northern Ireland, communities were born in one of two camps, the orange or the green, the Protestant or the Catholic. Both feel that they have religious claims to the truth. But the reality was that no matter what community you were born in and no matter what faith you chose to follow, Jesus Christ is looking for born-again believers and not religious fanatics or political disciples. I was brave and strong that night, with a presence I knew to be God's. The interesting thing was that all of those talks were recorded on little cassettes. And somehow, certainly not by my encouragement or doing, my father heard that talk and understood the context in which it was given. My mother told me that he listened to it in the living room of their tiny estate flat and that he left the room in tears, revealing later to my mother that he was proud of the stand I took. So in some way he came around to the strength needed to become a Christian, especially in an area like ours. He saw the courage needed to be a disciple of Jesus Christ, and appreciated the stand I took when faced with a looming threat against that Christian courage. He eventually died of lung cancer when he has 64. I miss him, for I wish that now, as a man, I could talk with him, in a way that I felt I never could back then. I wish I could reason and debate with him, maybe even laugh and come to a place of peace with him. But it is too late for that. Cancer is truly the curse of our generation.

My mother lived to see me marry, have children and become a missionary. She died just before I gained my first Degree. She would have loved to have seen that. She was a tiny woman with the greatest of hearts. Generous to a fault and fiercely protective of all her children, grandchildren and yes, great-grandchildren. She took ill in 2010 and was seemingly just about to be released from hospital when she took a sharp downward turn and me, Tulsi and the girls made it over from Germany to Northern Ireland just in time. I arrived at the Antrim Area Hospital at 8pm and held my mother's hand, just as I did with my father in his dying moments, until 8am the next morning when she slipped away. I had a wonderful relationship with my mother and live today without regrets in all that I was able to share with her. I miss her. But I truly believe that I will see her again. My sisters tell me that her last week in hospital was filled with talking about them and about life and about God.

*I had a wonderful relationship with my mother and live today without regrets in all that I was able to share with her.*

I believe that I have come to the end of my letter. Yes, it is a long one and yes, it may be different from what you might have expected. But I do hope you enjoyed it. It is dramatic at least. I started out by suggesting that life is a funny old thing. You will now understand why I said that.

I wonder what you think about all that I have shared with you? Maybe you think it is all a little too much, something you hadn't banked on and wish you had never started! I guess it's too late for that now. Maybe some of my story resonates with you and the sense of hope and purpose has translated a touch into your own story so far. Or maybe you have experienced what I truly hoped and have prayed that you would experience; the same experience I felt when I was listening to Sandra and Tracy in that living room. The same experience I felt when I was listening to Tommy on those Spring Sunday nights in that little Nissan Hut. The voice of another beyond the one that lies between the lines of this letter. A voice so straight and powerful that it reaches the very fibre of your soul and touches the very heart of your spirit. I do so pray that that is your experience.

As I sign off now, could I ask you to do something? Could I ask you to consider my story and perhaps place your own life in that little gospel hall, listening to the words that I have retraced for you? Could I ask you to think about your own response to the great mercy of God and think about where your own life is heading? Are you a Christian, a born-again believer in Jesus Christ? Are you assured of an eternity in Heaven and are sure of escaping the just punishment of Hell? It does not give me pleasure to speak of such things, but would I be a good steward of this message of the salvation of God if I were not to encourage entering into the blessings while avoiding experiencing the traumas of accepting and rejecting such a magnanimous offer of redemption?

> *I can honestly say that making the decision to give up my life for a life of following Jesus Christ is the single greatest thing I have ever done.*

I can honestly say that making the decision to give up my life for a life of following Jesus Christ is the single greatest thing I have ever done. Any of the blessings, the good fortune, the happy endings that I have experienced I can trace back to that Saturday evening knock at the door, to those meetings in that little hall and to that prayer of commitment in the tiny broom cupboard. Ultimately, I put it all down to the intervention of a God who cared enough to give his all for me, and who, in the process of time, called out to me while I was so hopelessly lost and moving towards an unhappy ending, one filled with potential brokenness and untold shattered dreams.

No, I have not become the world boxing champion or the new Martin Luther King. But what I have I am grateful for. A family of my own. A marriage I cherish. A purpose to live for. But most of all a Saviour I call both my Lord and my friend.

Yours Sincerely,

William.